Motivation Marvels

Dawn Gauvreau

authorHOUSE®

AuthorHouse™
1663 Liberty Drive
Bloomington, IN 47403
www.authorhouse.com
Phone: 1-800-839-8640

First published by AuthorHouse 5/13/2010

ISBN: 978-1-4389-7894-9 (e)
ISBN: 978-1-4389-7893-2 (sc)

Printed in the United States of America
Bloomington, Indiana

This book is printed on acid-free paper.

Motivation Marvels

Inside this book, you will find:

- Program Description

- Program Implementation

- Program Modifications

- Philosophy

- Forms:

- Assertive Discipline-Classroom Component

- Class Rules

- Checking Account Reward System

- Parent Sign off form

- Responsibility Report

- Reward Menu (Store List, Ticket Trade-In Chart)

- Weekly Progress Report

- And much more

What is *MOTIVATION* ???

Webster's definition of **motivation**: to provide with a motive; instigate; induce

Motivation: the act of motivating or providing an incentive

Motivational Research: in advertising and marketing, the use of sampling and psychoanalytical techniques to find out why people choose or reject a product or idea

Motive: a conscious or unconscious need, drive, etc. that incites a person to some action or behavior; incentive; goal

Motivation Marvels

A positive behavior management system geared to all ages and all levels in grades K – 12 that uses real life skills that encourage and entice students to do their best and reap the rewards of their hard work. This program uses real life tools that no kid can pass up.

The tools in this system are used in every day life. Students will learn life-long skills including check writing, budgeting, and saving.

Implementation and execution is very easy and blends well with just about any behavior system in place in a classroom.

Feel free to share your ideas and changes that work for you!

Thank you for your interest in this program.

For information or questions, contact:

Dawn Gauvreau

dawn.gauvreau@kcsdschools.net

birdlady5@sc.rr.com

What Motivation Marvels is all about

Motivation Marvels provides a way to hook, reel in, and get the results you want in the classroom while teaching real life skills. *Motivation Marvels* is both a behavior management system and a motivational tool.

The beauty of *Motivation Marvels* is that it is practical, motivational, functional, and adaptable to any grade or any level in regular education settings as well as most special education settings.

The only limits on this system are those an individual teacher imposes upon it.

The key to this system is the responsibility factor that is built into it. This program requires students to take responsibility for their behavior. If they are doing the right things, they are rewarded for it. If not, they see consequences that directly influence them.

Motivation Marvels behavior management system operates under the premise that in order for learning to take place all students must be actively engaged in the learning process and the teacher must have complete control and attention from the students in the class.

This system provides a quick, easy way to gain and maintain attention from your students while teaching them basic life skills.

Motivation Marvels uses functional life skills to entice students while educating them at the same time.

Motivation Marvels is the brainchild of years of trial and error behavior management. Through experimentation, I discovered some things that truly motivate all kids. I know, first hand, that this system works because I have used it from 4-year-old Language Concepts through high school. I have made some minor changes to meet the needs of the grade levels it was being used for, but everything else in the program remains the same.

As teachers, we are constantly competing for the attention of our students during classes. So many other things occupy their minds that we need to be as creative as we can as we hook and reel them in to what we have to say. *Motivation Marvels* is a tool that will help you do just that.

This program is user friendly and takes a minimal amount of time to familiarize yourself with the basic premises that govern it. *Motivation Marvels* comes complete with everything you will need to begin implementation in your classroom or school. Once you begin to use it, you may make changes that are appropriate to your specific setting. This kit allows for much flexibility within all levels from kindergarten through high school.

Why go the extra distance? Why a "stage production"?

Over the years gaining and maintaining student motivation has become increasingly more difficult. Teachers find themselves competing against so many factors such as interest levels, ability levels, outside hobbies/interests, part time jobs, and family obligations. Sadly, education seems to be less of a priority to some students enrolled in schools today.

This leads teachers to do one of two things: just continue doing what they have been doing knowing they will keep getting what they have been getting, or they can go the extra distance and find the one thing that will grab the interest of their class and motivate them to reach their maximum potential. Short of doing a stage show, teachers need to keep it real, lively, and interesting to keep students motivated and actively engaged.

This I know to be true: kids like rewards, kids like edibles, and kids like money. So...

With an extensive background of over three decades in Special Education, I have become a master of creativity. I was forced to think outside the box long before the box was popular. Thinking outside the box simply translates into "if it isn't working, stop doing it and do something else". The idea here is to let the student's reactions and responses lead your choices. You can quickly assess the success or failure of what you are doing by watching what is going on around you in the classroom.

Being flexible follows on the heels of being creative. If you have to stop doing something, you had better have a Plan B waiting in the wings. Some teachers have a hard time aborting a lesson or program in mid- stream because they think they need to see it through and complete it. Behavior programs/ reinforcement systems once started are often kept in place for the entire year even though they are not yielding the results hoped for at the onset. Even a lesson that is not working as planned should be aborted and something else used to replace it. The worst thing a teacher can do is to continue with a lesson, program, or reinforcement system if they know it is not working. You can be sure that if you can recognize that it is not working, so can those 10 to 20 pairs of eyes staring back at you everyday. Admitting that something is not working and will no longer be used can be a major teachable moment for kids. They can see that you too, make errors, mistakes, and need to sometimes stop, regroup, and try again. After all, isn't that what we tell them all the time? Besides, what better time to discuss the situation and let them know that you are constantly fine-tuning your class to guarantee that they get the best educational program every single day they are there. Depending on the grade level you teach, the explanations can be tweaked to make the most sense to your specific audience. My experiences have been that kids respond favorably to seeing you make a mistake, admit it, and then set about correcting it.

How the System works

Motivational Marvels is predicated on the belief that behavior management is necessary for learning to take place and motivation can inspire any student to behave.

This system incorporates the theory of assertive discipline in the classroom. To this theory, add the motivational component and you have all you need to successfully teach all day long.

There is a philosophy that explains how and why assertive discipline works in the classroom. This system incorporates rules of conduct through a classroom component that details consequences for breaking rules within the class. There can be as many levels as your grade level and students require. A very workable amount is usually between four and six.

The **Class Rules** and **Consequences** are posted in the class. Ample time to go over and explain these rules thoroughly must take place on day one. The **Consequences** are the **Classroom Component** part of the program. Depending on the grade level of your class, you can post them either way.

The next phase of this program introduces the ***Phoney Bucks. Phoney Bucks*** are just what the name implies. They are fake money that the students earn all day, every day. Further explanation for uses of **Phoney Bucks** will follow.

The Life Skills component of this system comes into play with the introduction of checks and check registers with older classes and basic savings with younger students.

From fourth grade on up you can introduce checks and check writing. Students can only spend their **Phoney Bucks** by correctly and accurately writing a check. They also must enter all **Phoney Bucks** deposits on the check registers correctly and accurately. Initially, this is the most time consuming part of this entire system. However, failure to take that time can result in teaching incorrect ways to record deposits and withdrawals as well as incorrect ways to fill out a check that can have devastating effects down the line. This program provides the necessary tools to practice check writing and maintaining a check register. It is amazing how quickly the students will catch on to this. The realistic, life skill appeal of being able to write a check like Mom or Dad is very powerful to students. Students love to go home and tell their parents they have a real checking account at school. I recommend using actual checks (starter checks photocopied) and actual registers so they students will be able to learn and transfer the skills they are acquiring when the have their own real checking accounts.

Lower grade levels can earn "Fun Time" tickets that also need to be saved in order to be redeemed.

High school students will usually use theirs as they earn them. Some like to save them for special rewards. If they do not redeem on the day they are earned, they still must record their deposit in their register in order to be able to spend them at a later date.

It is extremely important that you monitor all deposits and double check the math on both deposits and withdrawals to verify accuracy.

This will become less tedious as you and your students become more adept at working with the system.

Unfortunately, from time to time, you may also come across deposits that were never actually given. Careful scrutiny catches such incidences. This is, however; the exception, not the rule!

Using the *Phoney Bucks:*

There are no limits to what a student can do to earn **Phoney Bucks**. Below is just a sample list of the behaviors you can reward with **Phoney Bucks:**

Positive behavior in classes

Being on time to class

Turning in class work

Turning in homework

Answering questions in class

Bonus bucks for hard questions

Subject matter review

Helping someone without being asked

Returning signed papers/documents

Good behavior for a substitute

Good behavior in hallways, lunchroom, assemblies, etc.

Honor rolls (or any grade improvement)

100% on tests or class work

Being prepared for class (supplies)

Running teacher errands

Meeting goals in class subjects

Working hard/quietly in class

Keeping desk clean

Keeping locker organized

Getting good reports from other teachers

Trivia game review for upcoming tests

And anything else you can think of...

Suggestions way to use *Phoney Bucks* to reinforce positive behavior in your classroom:

I can stand in the front of my room, thumb through a stack of Phoney Bucks, and instantly gain the attention of my class. The talking stops and all eyes focus on me. I will often walk around the room and also just start placing **Phoney Bucks** on the desks of those who are quiet and waiting or quiet and working and within 10 seconds almost everyone else gets the picture and follows suit. I rarely have to say a word to get everyone's attention.

Phoney Bucks are passed out during a class or lesson for anything from good behavior to correct answers. Before the students leave to go to another class, I require they add their money earned into the check register and return their **Phoney Bucks** to me.

I do this for several reasons. First of all, I only have a limited amount of money. I reuse the dollars and preserve them by making them and then laminating them. They sit in a holder on my table all day. I also make a much smaller amount of $5.00 bills for those rare occasions when I really want to get someone's attention.

I also want them to record the money as they earn it so amounts are not forgotten or changed. If a student opts to do it later, I simply tell them that money not recorded as earned at that time cannot be recorded later. This may sound harsh but unless a situation occurs where there is truly no time, I do not deviate from this rule. My reason is that it is simply too hard to remember how much each person earned and make sure it is correctly recorded later. This system is meant to work with limited difficulty and not to take a lot of class time throughout the day to implement.

The amount of money you give out at any one time is directly related to the rewards you offer and how the students will be able to spend their money. The next section will talk about how students can redeem their **Phoney Bucks.**

Redeeming *Phoney Bucks*

The biggest drawback of this program is at the redemption point. If you are clever at getting things free for your class, this is where you will want to use that skill. It is rather expensive to supply the store, but well worth the trade off in expense to get the results you need and want in your class in order to be able to teach all day, every day.

I named my store "G-Mart" because my students call me Mrs. G. At the store students can make daily purchases for items ranging from school supplies to edibles. A copy of the contents of the store and the prices for each item is included in the Forms section. Here is where you would personalize your list to meet the individual needs in your class and within your budget. Some teachers may be fortunate enough to be able to ask for funding for this system and get it. Others just have to be thrifty shoppers; always looking for things on sale. My favorite is to buy items right after a holiday when they are 50 – 75% off! Kids do not mind if Easter was last week. They will still buy a chocolate bunny or jellybeans or a light up Bunny pen.

If you find yourself in a teaching situation where students often do not have classroom supplies, the store serves as a way for the kids to be able to get the pencils, paper, binders, erasers, etc. they need while feeling as if they bought it and not seeing it as a hand out. Again, I buy plenty of school supplies when they go on sale just before school begins each summer and stock up the store for the year. Kids must use their **Phoney Bucks** if they come to school without necessary supplies to do their job. **No excuses, just write the check!**

This part of the program really helps students understand the concept of responsibility and having to be prepared for their job every day. I find students are relieved to know that they can get paper, folders, pencils, etc. that they may have forgotten to avoid a detention from a teacher.

It is important to establish a set time to write checks each day, otherwise kids will want to write them all day long. If you only have students for one period, you will need to end class a couple minutes early to allow students to write a check. If you have students all day long, I usually allow twice a day; once before lunch if they want to purchase a snack to take to lunch and once at the end of the day. You will be able to decide what works best for your class. I also impose a dollar amount maximum per day.

Check registers and completely filled out checks must be presented together. Verify the math in the register, then make sure the check is correct. If there are any errors, they are sent back to be corrected first. Remember, without doing this more harm than good can result since they are learning the wrong way to do something that is a life skill.

Phoney Buck **Fundamentals**
(*Phoney* rhymes with Money)

There are a few basics to understand about **Phoney Bucks**. The first rule of thumb is no matter how bad yesterday was for a particular student, today is a new day, and everyone starts fresh.

Students can begin to earn their dollars at the beginning of the day. The teacher holds the discretion for whom, how much, and when dollars are doled out. **An important rule to remember and follow is once you give a dollar it can never be taken back!** Now, don't fret, there are some ways around that too.

Students who are not doing what they have been asked simply do not get a dollar when you walk around the room. They will quickly see that they were skipped over and usually that is enough to get them back on track. Sometimes a student will be having an extremely difficult day and will make comments about not caring about "those stupid *Phoney Bucks*", or may go as far as telling you where you can put them. However, they truly do care that they have been skipped over. During the tougher times, I may either ignore such comments or encourage the student to do whatever he or she needs to do to start earning their money too.

Some deviations with *Phoney Bucks*

I have worked in situations where I have had to send a student out of the classroom to regroup. I have been lucky enough to work with a cooperating teacher across the hall or in the next room who is willing to let my student sit there and process for a few moments. During the time my student is in the other room, he or she must fill out a **Responsibility Report**, which acts as their pass to reenter my class. Also, at the end of the class, they must pay what I call my "Inconvenience fee" for having to go to the other room. At this time they must write a check from their account for the fee. This teaches them that there is a consequence for their imposition upon the other teacher and the other class. Of course, depending on the type of infraction and behavior, this system does not work every time. It may require administration or SRO assistance if the student needs to leave the room.

Christmas Auction

The most popular part of this system is the Christmas Auction. This is a tremendously big hit with the students. Start talking up the auction in September and begin teasing the students by holding weekly "previews" of some of the items that will be available at the auction. Take out just two or three items each week at the preview. Be sure these items are things you know the students are interested in! Having an auction teaches kids about saving and budgeting— two very important life skills that go along with having money, managing a checking account, and being able to buy things you want.

If you see a student who spends every dollar he earns every day—which they can do— try to encourage and whet their appetite to save a little by showing them items they will have an opportunity to buy at the auction. Remember, we know friends and family members who do not save their money either, but spend it all living paycheck to paycheck. Although we may want more for them, we cannot really stop them. As a teacher, all you can do is try to explain why saving and budgeting is a good idea.

The auction is an incredible experience for any students. It is amazing to see how quickly students with money and math issues can catch on to how to bid and know how much they have spent and what they have left.

The best part is that the students will ask you how much particular items will cost and when you tell them that is up to them they will say things like, "Oh, that will just be a dollar or five dollars". However, as we practice our mock auction a week before the real one and they see how bidding really works, they change their mind completely about pricing.

The mock auction helps to ensure that all students fully understand how the process works and guarantees that all students will have an equal opportunity to participate.

In order to make it a learning experience for all students, you may want to keep a check on how much money everyone has as the time for the auction approaches. I try to give everyone an opportunity to have enough money to buy a few items at the auction. You may need to contrive some situations so students with little to no money may get a chance to fatten their account in time for the auction. Situations like putting a "random" sticker under a desk or chair for 200 **Phoney Bucks,** when in fact it was placed under a certain desk for someone who had very little money. Staging opportunities to equal out accounts helps students to fully buy into the program.

You should allow students to use calculators during the auction and have a few volunteers on hand to monitor students as they make their deductions to ensure accuracy.

Be advised that purchasing items for the auction can be costly! Explore ways to get items donated or to get assistance in purchasing them. Ask your principal, PTO, or send out "beg" letters to major corporations to help offset expenses.

Another idea to get your students to buy into the system more is to hold a design contest during the first week of school to adopt a new design for your own *Phoney Bucks.* Students will love having the opportunity to design the face of the money that will be used all year long. You can then run copies of the bills and laminate them. You might even change the design every marking period.

Poll your students that first week and see what they like. Buy those items for the store. If you class has a fondness for cookies, buy those. If no one likes Milky Way bars, there is really no sense in a bag of those. After all, you are trying to motivate your students by giving them things they like.

*Responsibility Report can be found in Forms section.

Modifications for early grades and high school students:

For early grades, the checking account system is replaced with "Fun Time" tickets. However, the basic premise is the same. The students earn their tickets for much the same reasons as they earned **Phoney Bucks**. They store their tickets in wallets they make and keep wallets in their desk throughout the year. Since the tickets are consumable, the students need to be reminded to put their names/initials on the back the minute they get them. The rule for "found" tickets on the floor without a name on them is "finder's keepers, loser's weepers".

Phoney Bucks can be used with the lower grades too. The checking account/check register component, however; would not be used. Young children love getting money as well as older students. You could have them put their dollars in their wallet that they would make. If you elect to use the tickets, a folder or a zipper pencil pouch would suffice.

The ticket or dollar trade in chart must be posted in several places around the room so the children have a visual reminder of what they can redeem their tickets to buy. It is much easier to fund a store at the elementary level since students in the kindergarten – third grade level. Dollar stores and Oriental Trading Company are a big help in finding affordable items and trinkets for the store. A sample trade in chart is included in the forms section.

Reinforcers that work well at this level include puffy/scratch and sniff/hologram stickers, awards, good notes home, pencils, erasers, being the classroom helper, office errand runner, cookies, candy, etc.

The Christmas auction may be modified at this grade level at the discretion of the teacher. Much work and preparation would need to be done to help the students understand the concept of delayed gratification and to help understand how to budget and save some tickets. The plus side would be that it would be much less expensive to fund an auction at this level.

Making the wallets should be a big production so the students understand the importance of keeping track of their tickets and having a safe place to keep them.

Teachers can choose to collect the wallets each day or let students keep them.

Harding House* makes an excellent product called "Good Time" tickets that have different animal pictures on them. They are relatively inexpensive and attractive to young children. You could also opt to go more cheaply and buy carnival tickets at Wal-Mart. However, the price difference is minimal and the students love the preprinted colorful pictures on the tickets. Ordering information for Harding House Publishers can be found below.

Harding House Publishers, Inc.

3426 West Palmetto Street

Florence, SC 29501

Email: support@hardinghouse.com

Toll-Free:1-800-662-2144

Toll-Free Fax: 1-888-661-2625

High School modifications:

High school modifications are pretty basic. Most high school students are interested in immediate reinforcement and will opt to use their money as they earn it buying items such a small candy, chips, sodas, or a pack of gum.

The checks and register component still applies and should be used. When I used this program with my high school students, I was one of the few classes that never had tardy students. Of course, the reason was I "paid" my students for being on time, but it worked!

A concern about using this system with high school students was wondering how they would respond to it. That fear was quickly suppressed and the students jumped on board almost immediately. A few never bought into it, but at this age, that is their choice. Here again, the key is to sweeten the pot with tempting reinforcers you know they are interested in.

You also alter the list of things they are reinforced for accordingly including things such as signed papers, homework, attendance, reporting to class on time etc. Again, you determine the limits on your system.

At both the middle school and high school level, I set a daily spending limit to help preserve inventory as well as giving an opportunity for all who may choose to make a purchase. The limit is usually the price of two big treat items. In my store, Sweet Treats (big ones) were $50 each so our class limit was $100 per day for edibles.

Foundations and Forms of the Program

The following section consists of the foundation of this behavior management system. Included are several forms that can be used to hand out at the beginning of the year to inform and explain the system to parents. There is also a Parent Sign Off page that parents sign indicating an understanding of and a willingness to support this system.

Classroom Component

The classroom Component section can be used and modified according to the grade level you teach. It is extremely important that these rules are explained and discussed on the first day of school. Students need to understand rules and consequences prior to having them be enforced.

The example was used in a middle school setting.

Class Rules

This page is posted in the class in a more appealing, colorful format. Again, on the first day of school, each student received their own copy and a copy is signed by everyone in the class and posted on the wall for the year. This serves to remind students who may temporarily forget they discussed, signed, and agrees to abide by specific rules determined on the first day of school.

Checking Account Reward System

This sheet goes home along with the Philosophy to explain to parents what is going on in their child's class. Any part may be modified to meet specific grade level needs.

Parent Sign Off

This sign off is critical because it commits parents, as well as students, to the program. Parents have a very clear understanding of what is going on in the class and can converse with their child about their money, savings, or spending.

Responsibility Report

This report is an optional component. It can be used with students as a processing instrument if you give them some positive time-out to process what happened. They use the form to write about the situation. It can also be used with the student to sit down with them and go through it verbally after they have calmed down. This option will also work if you have students with writing issues.

I always offer **Phoney Bucks** to students for the completion of this form. It is important for the student to process what happened and reflect on future behavior. If you elect to send it home for a parent signature, it would be better to award the **Phoney Bucks** after it comes back signed.

Store Price List

I strategically place several price lists around the classroom so students are constantly aware of what is for sale and the cost of each item.

One variation on this list is that prices can be increased each marking period to raise the level of student achievement required for compensation. In the beginning, it is very important to make sure rewards are attainable for every student in order to have them buy into the program.

School supply prices remain constant throughout the year. These are available for kids who seem to come to school unprepared every day. They need to learn about consequences and by having the opportunity to buy what they need. They are also learning about being responsible and making sure they have the tools they need to do their job.

Treats and luxury items such as Free Time, or Deadline Extension certificates*which can be increased each quarter in an attempt to wean students from such purchases.

*Deadline Extension Passes replace the idea of a Homework Pass because it gives students extra time to turn in a specific assignment instead of letting them think it was not important enough to do at all as with a Homework Pass.

Weekly Progress Reports

Optional Weekly Progress Reports sent home continually keep parents abreast of student progress on a weekly basis. I heavily reward the weekly return of these documents with **Phoney Bucks**.

Surprisingly, it is very rare not to get a report returned. This form serves to make parent conferences and report card time much less stressful. With weekly parent signatures, report grades are no longer a surprise. Parents are aware throughout the nine weeks as to how their child is progressing.

These reports remain on file throughout the year.

K- 3 Ticket Trade-In Chart

With the lower levels it is recommended to use the Fun Time Tickets in place of dollars. Students will earn tickets in the same fashion and spend them accordingly. They need to be encouraged to put their name on the back of their tickets as they earn them in case they fall onto the floor or are left on top of their desk.

Wallets or folders can be made in class to store the tickets in. Zippered pencil pouches also work well for storage and fit easily in desks.

Trade in chart can include any motivating items and can include basic school supplies such as pencils erasers or paper. Dollar stores are a great place to buy rewards that are reasonably priced. Stickers, good notes home, and of course, small candy treats remain among the favorite items of most young children.

Construction of this trade in chart needs to be big, bright, and colorful. It is recommended to include the actual number of tickets next to the item on the chart so children can see exactly what they need for a given item.

If you prefer to use dollars instead of the tickets in the early grades, simply place the number of dollars next to each item on the chart. The only major difference from using money in K-3 and in the upper grades is the use of the checking account. I have successfully used a checking account in grades 4 and up.

The **Philosophy** page explains the foundation of the assertive discipline program. This may be used to send home to parents at the beginning of the school year. The rules of conduct may be modified according to the grade level being taught.

Parents tend to support programs in the classroom when they are aware of them prior to a problem arising. Parents are also a great resource to go to in order to get supplies and trinkets to include in your store.

The charts and forms that follow were used in middle school setting. Modifying the content of any forms may be necessary depending on the age and grade taught.

Philosophy

In an effort to make the school year a success for everyone in my room, I have developed an assertive discipline program that will be in effect this year.

Assertive discipline promotes an atmosphere in which learning is valued and people respected, where incentive is provided for each student to perform to the best of his or her abilities, and teachers and students work together to fulfill the educational aspirations of children, teachers, parents, and members of the community.

Within this disciplined setting students and teachers strive for high academic standards. Students and staff recognize that teaching and learning entail effort and hard work as well as fun. Students who disrupt the educational process will be addressed fairly, firmly, and promptly for the safety and welfare of others.

It is when students can demonstrate self-discipline and act as responsible community members that teachers can provide an enjoyable educational setting, one that is safe, comfortable, rewarding, and respectful of each student as an individual.

Rules of Conduct

1. Respectfully listen to whoever is speaking and raise your hand to speak.

2. Use acceptable language in our classroom.

3. Keep hands, feet, and objects to yourself at all times.

4. Come to school prepared every day.

Assertive Discipline Program—Classroom Component

❖ 1st Occurrence- Verbal Warning

❖ 2nd Occurrence- Lunch Detention/ Dollar(s) Withheld

❖ 3rd Occurrence~ Responsibility Report

(Student will write what the problem is and offer acceptable ways to solve it in the future) This will be sent home to be signed and returned the next day. Failure to complete this form will be treated as a Level Two offense and will receive an immediate written referral.

OR

❖ - Conference with student, teacher, and parent and after school detention

❖ 4th Occurrence~ Referral and/or meeting with student and Principal, Assistant principal, and/or guidance)

Class Rules

Respectfully listen to whoever is speaking and raise your hand to speak

Use acceptable language in our classroom

Keep hands, feet, and objects to yourself

Come to school prepared daily

Consequences

Verbal reminder

Lunch detention/Dollar Deduction

Responsibility Report (call home with note to be signed)

Parent Conference/After School Detention

Principal/ Assistant Principal/SRO/Guidance

Remember: Being a member of this class is a privilege. If you abuse that privilege, you will lose it and be removed from the class until you can participate appropriately in here.

August 20__

Checking Account Reward System

You will have your own checking account this year.

You will be responsible for learning how to write checks and how to record and enter transactions in your check register. You will earn ***Phoney Bucks*** each day for anything from being on time to turning in homework, to doing something nice for someone else, to giving a correct answer in class, etc.

At the end of each class you will count your ***Phoney Bucks*** you have earned and enter it into your check register. Since we will be using actual checks you will have to correctly fill out your check if you choose to spend any or all of your earned money. We will go over the procedure for writing checks and entering transactions in your check register before you begin writing your checks.

You will be able to buy items such as Sweet Treats (mini-sized candy treats, cookies, box drinks, etc.), lead pencils, fancy # 2 pencils, regular #2 pencils or pens, loose-leaf paper, spiral notebooks, pocket folders, passes for 15 minutes of free time, deadline extension certificates, and many other things. I will post a list of things that can be purchased for the first semester. You will be able to write your check at the end of class or you may just keep the money until you choose to buy a particular item. Watch for details about our exciting Christmas Auction!!!

At the beginning of the second semester, the prices for each item will increase thus requiring you to have to work harder to earn your luxury items.

Good luck!   Have fun!
Plan ahead!

Save well and spend wisely!!!

Your name
Your School
Your grade

August 20

I have received the assertive discipline program and classroom guidelines and policies that my child will be participating in this year. I understand that the program has been established to promote a positive learning environment in the classroom. I have read it, discussed it with my child, and will work with you in supporting it.

_____

Parent's Signature

(Your) SCHOOL
RESPONSIBILITY REPORT

Student _____

Date _____

Teacher _____

Class _____

Instructions:
Answer each of the questions clearly and in complete sentences.

1. What rule did you break?

2. Who was bothered when you broke this rule?

3. What should you have done instead?

4. What will you do in the future?

Please give this clipboard back to your teacher if you are finished and can

agree to follow the classroom expectations.

Student Signature _____

Teacher signature _____

Parent Signature _____

Please return this signed to your teacher tomorrow.

Thank you.

G~MART

Leads- 3 pieces	15 Dollars
Number 2 Pencil	5 Dollars
Sweet Treat (small)	30 Dollars
Agenda Page	40 Dollars
Lead Pencils	40 Dollars
Loose Leaf Paper, Spiral Notebook, Folders	40 Dollars
Snack (large)	50 Dollars
15 minutes of free time	45 Dollars
Deadline Extension Certificate	50 Dollars
Nintendo (20 minutes)	75 Dollars

Weekly Progress Report   **Week of_____**

Student:

GRADES:	Class work	Homework	Tests
Language Arts			
Math			
A.R. Reading:			

Met Goal _____   Did not meet goal _____
Comments:

"N/A" means it does not apply to the student at this time.
"IC" means Incomplete and the student has not turned in this assignment.

Behavior:

Comments:

Teacher: _____ **Date:** _____

Parent Signature: _____ **Date:** _____

Feel free to make any comments on the back of this page.

Checks, Check Registers, and *Phoney Bucks*

Checks

It is recommended to use actual checks with this system. Banks will usually give out a starter pack free of charge. The actual checks in this starter pack can be photocopied to use with your class. Prior to making copies of the checks, you must make a set for each child with their name and address written in on the top left hand corner of the check. An original should be kept for making copies as the student needs more checks. The numbers on each check must also be written in on the check.

Check Registers

Check registers can also be obtained from a local bank. If you are able to obtain enough registers, students can just use the register. If not, you can open up a register make a photocopy and use that as a page in their checking account folder.

It is suggested to copy four checks per page. Usually one sheet (four checks) is all that goes in the file folder at a time.

If you use a manila file folder, the left side can have the checks stapled in and the right side can have the register stapled there. When I use actual registers, I buy library card pocket holders and place those in the middle of the right hand side of the file folder and the students can place their actual register inside to avoid it from falling out of the folder.

During the first several days of school, students need to practicing writing checks correctly and using the check register correctly. You will be amazed at how quickly they will catch on and be able to write checks just like adults.

It is very important that they learn the correct way to do this right from the start.

Students will staple a correctly filled out check under their sheet of checks in the file folder to use as reference when they are filling out those beginning checks. This cuts down on the help they will need at the start. I also have students write number words they will frequently use under their check register. I am adamant that their checks are correct and that include spelling errors.

Any errors in a check they attempt to turn in must be corrected on the spot to avoid the students from learning how to fill out checks incorrectly.

Phoney Bucks

As stated earlier, the dollars should be made on colored construction paper and laminated for longevity. Each dollar amount should be made on a different colored piece of paper to avoid confusion in values.

Students can feel more a part of this system if you have a design contest to pick the design or face to go on your dollars. The winning design can be used for the year or changed each marking period.